LOAD PLANS & LEADERSHIP

LOAD PLANS & LEADERSHIP

Margin for Error: Minimal

WHAT WORKS. WHAT DOESN'T. WHAT LEADERS GET WRONG.

Todd Everett Wende

Command Master Chief, U.S. Navy (Ret.)

ISBN: 979-8-9953790-1-0

Published by

KaTiga Advisory Group

Eastland, Texas, USA

First Edition

Printed in the United States of America

For bulk orders, speaking engagements, or organizational inquiries, contact:

info@katigaadvisory.com

The greatest gift of leadership
is building a team
that wants each other to win.

For Kailey and Tiga -

Everything in these pages was shaped by the years I spent trying to learn how to lead people well.

But the most important thing I have ever been is your father.

Author's Note

This is not a leadership textbook.

It is not based on academic theory, corporate consulting models, or research studies. The lessons in this book were learned on the deckplates.

For thirty years, I served in the United States Navy, eventually retiring as a Command Master Chief. Most of that time was spent in the Indo-Pacific, working alongside sailors responsible for real missions, real responsibility, and real consequences.

Leadership in that environment does not happen in classrooms. It happens during long deployments, late-night conversations, difficult decisions, and moments when someone younger than you walks into your office needing guidance.

Over time, I began to notice something important. The lessons that shaped the best leaders were rarely the ones written in manuals.

They came from small moments.

A conversation that changed someone's perspective.
A simple phrase that captured a leadership truth.
An experience that showed people something more clearly than a lecture ever could.

Many of the stories in this book come from moments like that.

Later in my career, after transitioning into the corporate world, I realized something else. The leadership challenges were remarkably similar.

Different uniforms.
Different terminology.
Different meeting rooms.

But the same human dynamics.

Organizations still struggled with decision speed. Leaders still created unnecessary rules. People still optimized for appearances instead of outcomes. And teams still relied on trust, judgment, and personal responsibility far more than any policy manual could explain.

That was the moment everything connected.

The environment changes.
The language changes.
But leadership does not.

This book captures the lessons that became clear along the way. They are not presented as perfect answers. They are observations from a career spent watching leadership succeed, fail, and evolve in real environments.

If the stories are useful, it will not be because they provide a formula. It will be because leadership, at its core, is simpler than we often make it.

Foreword

By Justin Banz

I had the opportunity to serve with Todd at HSM-51, where I saw firsthand his ability to bring clarity to complex situations and lead in environments where decisions mattered. I also had the opportunity to serve with him earlier in our Navy careers aboard the USS Chancellorsville, when he was a Hospital Corpsman Chief and I was a Lieutenant leading a Helo detachment. That perspective—serving together first as HMC and LT, and later as part of a squadron leadership team—gave me a unique view of how he leads and how that leadership evolves with experience. In operational settings where time is limited and the margin for error is small, that kind of leadership makes a real difference.

The lessons in this book reflect that same approach—practical, direct, and grounded in real-world experience. Todd writes about leadership the way he practiced it: focused on what works, not what sounds good in theory. He understands that effective leadership is not about adding complexity, but about reducing friction so teams can move quickly, make sound decisions, and accomplish the mission.

During our time working together, Todd consistently balanced mission requirements with the needs of his people. He was willing to challenge assumptions, simplify processes, and make decisions that improved outcomes—not just in the short term, but across the organization. That balance between execution and people is what separates good leaders from effective ones.

While his experience comes from the Navy, the principles in this book—clarity, accountability, trust, and decisiveness—apply in any organization. This is a perspective shaped by experience, and one that leaders at every level can learn from.

Justin Banz
Captain, U.S. Navy (Ret.)

Chapter 1
The First Real Responsibility

There are moments in life when responsibility stops being theoretical and becomes real.

In the Navy, those moments usually arrive quietly.

No ceremony.
No announcement.

Just a situation where people are looking at you for the answer, and you realize there isn't anyone else left to ask.

I experienced that moment early in my career while serving as an Independent Duty Corpsman.

Most people outside the Navy have never heard that term. Even inside the military, many sailors only understand part of what it means.

On small ships, the Independent Duty Corpsman—often called an IDC or "Doc" —is the entire medical department.

Doctor.
Nurse.
Pharmacist.
Medic.
Sanitation inspector.
Sometimes counselor.
Sometimes chaplain.

And occasionally, the only person standing between a sailor and a very bad outcome. On a ship, you quickly learn a simple truth: it cannot sail without the Captain—and it cannot safely operate or get underway without the IDC.

That responsibility becomes real the first time a sailor walks into sick call with a problem that doesn't have an obvious answer.

Because in that moment, there is no hospital down the corridor. There is no attending physician two doors away.

There is just you.

And a sailor who trusts you to figure out what comes next.

When I first entered the Navy, I didn't fully understand how much responsibility the role would eventually carry. Like most young sailors, I was focused on learning my job and proving that I belonged.

The military is full of talented people who expect competence. If you want to be taken seriously, you have to demonstrate quickly that you can handle the work.

So the early years were filled with training, certifications, and the daily rhythm of operational life.

Long hours.
Constant learning.
A steady stream of practical experience.

Over time, those experiences accumulate. You begin recognizing patterns—symptoms that signal something minor, and symptoms that signal something more serious. You develop a kind of situational awareness that only comes from seeing the same types of problems repeatedly.

But nothing fully prepares you for the moment when you realize the system is relying on you.

Not just your knowledge.

Your judgment.

And judgment is a different kind of responsibility.

Knowledge can be memorized.
Judgment has to be earned.

One of the realities of serving on smaller ships is that resources are limited. The Navy operates across the globe, often in places where immediate medical evacuation is impossible.

Ships may be hundreds or thousands of miles from the nearest hospital. Weather may delay flights. Operational requirements may prevent a ship from changing course.

All of that means the person responsible for medical decisions onboard must often act independently.

That independence is both empowering and intimidating. But independence doesn't mean you're alone.

On that ship, I had a junior corpsman—Vincent "Gonzo" Gonzales—who was an integral part of the medical team. Loyal. Reliable. The kind of sailor you trust without hesitation. He was still learning, still building experience, but he showed up every day ready to work and ready to take care of people.

That matters more than people think.

Because even when the final decision is yours, the team around you makes that decision stronger.

There are times when you can consult with doctors over radio or satellite communications. But there are also moments when communication delays or operational conditions force you to act before guidance arrives.

Those are the moments that define leadership more than any training manual.

I remember an early situation where a sailor arrived with symptoms that could have easily been dismissed as minor.

Fatigue.
Discomfort.
Nothing dramatic.

But something didn't sit right.

When you work in medicine long enough, you develop instincts about when something deserves closer attention. The symptoms alone didn't tell the full story.

But the sailor's demeanor did.

People often reveal more through behavior than through words. You could see the discomfort behind the casual description.

And that's where responsibility becomes real.

Do you treat it as routine and move on?
Or do you slow down, ask more questions, and dig deeper—even if it disrupts the schedule?

That moment might sound small on paper.

But those decisions matter.

Because sailors trust the person wearing that medical insignia. They assume someone is paying attention. They assume someone will take their concerns seriously. And once you recognize that trust, you start approaching the role differently.

Responsibility isn't about authority.

It's about protecting the people who rely on your judgment.

Over time, I began noticing something else about leadership.

People are always watching.

Not just the decisions you make, but how you make them.

How you treat someone who walks into your workspace.
How seriously you listen.
Whether you appear rushed or patient.

Whether you treat junior sailors with the same respect as senior personnel.

Those behaviors send signals.

A sailor who feels respected will speak up earlier when something is wrong. A sailor who feels dismissed may stay quiet until a small problem becomes something much larger.

Leadership lives inside those small interactions.

Not the dramatic moments.

The quiet ones.

The conversation at the door.
The decision to pause and listen.
The willingness to ask one more question.

Those choices build trust over time.

And trust is the foundation of every effective team.

The Navy teaches technical competence extremely well. Training pipelines exist for nearly every skill required to operate ships, aircraft, and logistics systems around the world.

But leadership cannot be fully taught in a classroom.

It develops through experience.

Through responsibility.

Through moments where people rely on you and you realize the outcome will be shaped by the decision you make next.

That realization changes how you approach your work.

You start thinking less about tasks and more about the people behind them.

The sailors working long hours.
The junior personnel trying to build careers.
The families back home trusting that their loved ones are being taken care of.

Leadership means carrying a portion of that responsibility.

Not because you asked for it.

But because the role requires it.

There is another part of responsibility people don't talk about— the quiet pressure that comes with realizing people trust your judgment.

Early in your career, authority feels abstract. Decisions come from somewhere higher in the chain of command. You execute tasks. You learn the system.

But eventually, someone looks at you and asks a question that no one else is going to answer.

And you realize the decision belongs to you. That realization changes everything. Because responsibility carries a weight that authority alone does not. Authority can be given.

Responsibility must be carried.

Leadership Lesson

The first real moment of leadership rarely arrives with a promotion.

More often, it appears quietly—when someone turns to you for guidance and you realize the answer depends on your judgment.

That moment changes how leaders see their role.

The focus shifts from completing tasks to carrying responsibility for people.

Authority can be assigned by rank or title. Responsibility must be accepted.

The strongest leaders slow down, ask better questions, and pay attention to the people affected by their decisions.

Leadership begins the moment someone recognizes that their choices carry consequences for others.

The Corporate Mirror

The same dynamic appears constantly in corporate environments.

Many professionals believe leadership begins with a title. They assume authority must come first before they can lead.

In reality, responsibility appears much earlier.

It shows up when a project encounters a problem and someone steps forward to take ownership. It shows up when a team looks for direction and one person begins asking the questions that move the conversation forward.

People notice.

Just as sailors observe the leaders around them, corporate teams watch closely to see how individuals respond when decisions become difficult. Over time, those observations shape credibility.

People begin to trust the individuals who consistently take responsibility, communicate honestly, and focus on solving problems rather than avoiding them.

Titles may define authority, but behavior defines leadership.

And just like in the Navy, the leaders people follow most naturally are often the ones who accepted responsibility long before they were officially placed in charge.

Chapter 2
The Popcorn Machine

When people think about leadership in the military, they usually imagine something formal.

Orders being given.
Meetings with senior leaders.
Serious conversations about mission readiness and operational priorities.

Those things absolutely exist.

But some of the most important leadership moments happen in places that don't look like leadership at all.

For me, one of those places involved a popcorn machine sitting in the corner of an office at NAVSUP Yokosuka.

When I first moved into the Command Master Chief office there, the machine was already in the room. It wasn't something I brought in or installed myself. It had simply been sitting there, unused, like a relic from some previous time.

Most people probably didn't even notice it anymore.

Offices tend to accumulate things like that—items that once had a purpose but eventually fade into the background of daily routine.

The popcorn machine was one of those things.

At some point early on, I decided to clean it up and use it.

Not because I had some carefully designed leadership initiative in mind.

Honestly, I just thought it might be a nice thing to have around.

So I bought supplies.

Popcorn kernels.
Oil.
A few seasonings.

Before long, I had worked out a blend that people started referring to as the "CMC mix."

Nothing fancy.

Just the right combination that made people come back for another bag.

The first few times I made popcorn, not many people noticed.

NAVSUP Yokosuka is a large organization with sailors, civilians, and contractors moving between meetings, offices, and operational responsibilities. Most people are busy.

But eventually the smell started drifting down the hallway.

And if you've ever walked past fresh popcorn being made, you know how hard it is to ignore.

One sailor stuck his head in the door and asked if he could grab a bag.

"Of course."

A few minutes later, someone else stopped by.

Then another.

Soon a pattern began to form.

People walking past would smell popcorn and poke their heads into the office.

"CMC, you making popcorn?"
"Yeah."
"Mind if I grab some?"
"Help yourself."

Those conversations rarely lasted more than a few minutes.

But that was never the point.

What started happening was something much more important.

Sailors began lingering.

At first they would grab popcorn and leave.

Then they started staying for a moment.

A short conversation.
A quick question.
A comment about something happening in their shop.

Over time, those small interactions became part of the rhythm of the command.

Someone walking past would smell popcorn and say to a coworker, "CMC's making popcorn," and before long a couple of them would be standing in the office talking for a few minutes.

Sometimes they asked questions.
Sometimes they just talked about life.
Sometimes they just enjoyed the break.

But those few minutes created something that formal leadership spaces often struggle to achieve.

Approachability.

Senior leadership offices can be intimidating places.

For junior sailors, walking into a Command Master Chief's office can feel like a trip to the principal's office. It usually means something serious is happening.

So people avoid those spaces unless they absolutely have to enter them.

The popcorn machine changed that dynamic.

Suddenly the office felt different.

Not informal.

But human.

Sailors realized they could step into the space without it being a formal event. They could talk for a few minutes, ask a question, or just say hello.

Over time, the popcorn itself became a small tradition.

Sailors would stop by and ask if I had the special mix that day.

Some joked it was the best part of the building.

Others simply enjoyed the break from routine.

But the most important part was never the popcorn.

It was the interaction.

The few minutes where rank faded into the background and people talked like human beings.

The Khaki Reactions

One thing I always noticed when the popcorn machine was running was the reaction from other senior enlisted leaders.

Occasionally, other Command Master Chiefs or khakis from visiting commands would stop by the office. They would walk in expecting the normal environment—quiet, formal, predictable.

Instead, they saw sailors standing around with bags of popcorn talking to the Command Master Chief.

You could see the reaction immediately.

That split-second look.

Part disbelief.
Part confusion.
Sometimes even a little bit of disgust.

You didn't have to ask what they were thinking.

It was written all over their faces.

This isn't how this office is supposed to look.

To them, the CMC office should feel serious. Controlled. A place sailors only enter when something important is happening.

Seeing junior sailors casually standing there eating popcorn didn't fit that image.

But I never cared what it looked like.

Because I understood what was actually happening.

Sailors were comfortable enough to walk into the office.

They were talking.

They were asking questions.

They were connecting with someone in senior leadership without feeling like they were crossing an invisible line.

That kind of access matters more than appearances ever will.

Leadership is not about maintaining distance.

It's about building trust.

And trust is built through conversation, not intimidation.

If a few bags of popcorn made that easier, I was perfectly fine with it.

Eventually my tour ended and I transferred.

Like every command, new leadership came in and things changed.

Not long after I left, the popcorn machine disappeared.

Apparently someone decided it didn't look professional enough.

I wasn't surprised.

Organizations often default back to what feels safe and familiar.

But what always stood out to me was what happened when I came back to visit.

After I retired, I would occasionally stop by NAVSUP Yokosuka.

And almost every time, the same thing happened.

Some sailor who had been there during my tour would recognize me, smile, and say:

"CMC… we miss the popcorn."

It happened so often it became a running joke.

But they weren't really talking about the popcorn.

They were talking about the atmosphere.

They were talking about the conversations.

They were talking about the feeling that the Command Master Chief's office was a place where they could walk in and talk to someone who actually wanted to hear what they had to say.

And that was always the real point.

Not the machine.

Not the popcorn.

The connection.

Leadership Lesson

Leadership is often communicated through small signals rather than formal directives.

When leaders create environments where people feel comfortable engaging, information flows more naturally and trust develops more quickly.

Approachability does not weaken authority.

It strengthens it.

Because people who feel comfortable speaking with leaders are far more likely to share concerns, ideas, and observations that help the organization improve.

Effective leaders understand that culture is shaped by everyday interactions. Not just formal meetings.

The atmosphere leaders create determines whether people speak up or stay silent.

The Corporate Mirror

The same dynamic appears in corporate environments, although it often looks different.

Many leaders unintentionally create distance between themselves and their teams.

Corner offices.
Closed doors.
Packed schedules.
Layers of management.

None of these things are inherently wrong, but they can create environments where communication becomes filtered.

Information moves through multiple layers before reaching decision-makers. By the time problems reach senior leadership, they are often larger and more complicated than they needed to be.

The most effective leaders understand the value of informal interaction.

They create space for casual conversations. They remain visible. They spend time where the work is actually happening.

These moments allow leaders to hear what people are really experiencing.

Just like the popcorn machine created an unexpected space for conversation, effective leaders find simple ways to encourage informal dialogue.

A few minutes of unscheduled interaction can reveal more about an organization than an hour-long briefing.

Because people speak more honestly when the environment feels human.

In both military and corporate environments, the lesson is the same.

Leadership influence does not come only from authority. It comes from connection.

And sometimes, that connection begins with something as simple as a bag of popcorn.

Chapter 3
The Liberty Plan

One of the most interesting leadership lessons I ever experienced started with something that seemed completely reasonable on the surface.

A liberty policy.

In the Navy, liberty policies are meant to protect sailors. They exist to reduce risk, maintain accountability, and prevent situations that can turn into disciplinary problems.

Every command has some version of them.

Curfews.
Buddy systems.
Restrictions on certain areas.

Rules designed to make sure sailors stay safe when they go out into foreign ports.

In theory, those policies make sense.

But sometimes leadership policies drift into a strange territory where the rule itself becomes more important than the reality it is supposed to address.

And when that happens, the policy starts creating problems instead of solving them.

I remember sitting in a leadership meeting when one of these policies came up for discussion.

At the time, the command had a rule that sailors going on liberty had to travel in groups of four.

Not two.

Four.

And one of those four sailors had to agree not to drink.

On paper, the idea sounded responsible.

Accountability.
Safety.
Risk management.

All the right words.

But the moment I heard the explanation, something didn't sit right.

Because leadership decisions cannot be evaluated only on their intentions. They have to be evaluated on whether they make sense in the real world.

And this rule didn't pass that test.

For one thing, it assumed that four sailors would always be available to go out together. Anyone who has spent time in the Navy knows that isn't always the case.

Schedules don't align that cleanly.
People get off watch at different times.
Some sailors just want to grab dinner or walk around town for an hour.

Requiring four people for something that simple created a logistical problem that didn't reflect reality. But the part that really stood out was the requirement that one of the four sailors had to remain sober.

That meant every liberty group needed a designated non-drinker.

Which raised a simple question.

Who volunteers for that role every time?

Sailors are smart. They understand rules quickly. And when rules feel unrealistic, people begin finding ways around them.

That's human nature.

So I asked a question in the meeting.

"What problem are we actually trying to solve?"

There was a moment of silence.

Someone repeated the explanation about safety and accountability.

I nodded.

That part made sense.

But then I asked the follow-up question that really mattered.

"Do we honestly believe sailors are going to follow this rule exactly the way it's written?"

Because leadership policies only work when they reflect human behavior.

Rules that ignore reality don't create discipline. They create workarounds. And workarounds slowly erode trust between leaders and the people they lead.

I remember looking around the room and offering an example.

"Let's say I'm a single E-9," I said.
"And I decide I want to go on a date tonight."

"Am I required to bring three other sailors with me and designate one of them as the non-drinker?"

The room laughed.

Because everyone immediately understood the point.

The rule sounded reasonable when applied to groups of junior sailors heading out for a night of drinking.

But the moment you applied the same logic to a senior leader, it sounded ridiculous.

That disconnect revealed the deeper issue.

The rule was built around control, not judgment.

Leadership often operates in that tension.

Control versus trust.

Control feels safer.
Control feels measurable.
Control produces policies that look good on paper.

But control has limits.

Organizations that rely too heavily on control eventually create environments where people stop using judgment.

They follow the rule.

Even when the rule no longer makes sense.

Trust, on the other hand, requires something different.

It requires leaders to accept that individuals will sometimes make mistakes.

But it also recognizes that people develop judgment only when they are allowed to exercise it.

The liberty rule had crossed the line into control for the sake of control.

It assumed sailors could not be trusted to manage their own behavior unless a rigid structure forced accountability.

That assumption might feel safe to leaders.

But it sends a clear signal to the people being led.

You are not trusted.

And when people believe they are not trusted, their behavior reflects that belief.

They comply with the letter of the rule while quietly working around its intent.

Eventually, the conversation in the meeting began to shift.

Someone acknowledged that the rule might be difficult to enforce.

Another leader admitted that sailors probably weren't following it exactly as written.

Once that realization surfaced, the policy started to unravel.

Because the worst kind of rule in any organization is a rule everyone knows is unrealistic.

Those rules create a culture of quiet dishonesty.

People pretend to follow them. Leaders pretend they are effective. And everyone understands the truth but avoids saying it out loud.

Good leadership requires confronting those moments honestly.

Policies should reflect reality.

They should encourage responsible behavior rather than forcing artificial compliance.

Eventually, the liberty policy was adjusted.

Not eliminated, but simplified.

The focus shifted toward accountability and responsible decision-making rather than rigid numerical requirements.

And something interesting happened.

Sailors didn't suddenly start behaving recklessly. In fact, many handled liberty more responsibly once the policy reflected basic common sense. Because when people feel trusted, they often rise to that expectation.

Leadership is not about eliminating risk.

That is impossible.

Leadership is about managing risk intelligently while still treating people like adults. The liberty policy meeting reinforced something I had been noticing throughout my career.

Leaders sometimes create rules that make them feel safer rather than rules that actually improve behavior.

And those are not the same thing.

Leadership Lesson

Rules are useful tools, but they cannot replace judgment.

When policies become disconnected from real-world behavior, they often create the opposite effect of what leaders intended.

Instead of improving discipline, unrealistic rules encourage people to find ways around them.

Effective leaders design policies that reflect how people actually behave.

They balance accountability with trust.

They understand that people develop judgment only when they are allowed to exercise it.

Leadership is not about controlling every decision.

It is about creating an environment where responsible decisions become the natural choice.

The Corporate Mirror

Corporate organizations face the same tension between trust and control.

Companies create detailed policies designed to reduce risk and standardize behavior.

Expense rules.
Approval chains.
Travel restrictions.
Process checklists.

Each of these usually begins with a reasonable intention.

But over time, layers accumulate.

New requirements are added after each problem. Additional approvals are inserted to prevent mistakes.

Eventually, employees find themselves navigating systems that feel increasingly disconnected from reality.

Just like sailors dealing with unrealistic liberty policies, employees adapt.

They find workarounds.

They create unofficial shortcuts.

They learn which rules are enforced and which exist only on paper.

When that happens, organizations drift into a culture where compliance becomes performative.

People follow the visible steps of the process while working around the parts that slow progress.

The most effective leaders recognize this pattern early.

Instead of adding more rules, they step back and ask a simpler question.

Does this policy actually help people do their jobs better?

If the answer is no, the policy needs to change.

Trust does not eliminate accountability.

But it recognizes that responsible adults perform better when they are treated like responsible adults.

The best organizations find the balance between structure and judgment.

And just like in the Navy, the strongest leaders understand that sometimes the smartest rule is the one that trusts people to use their heads.

Chapter 4
When Leaders Start Celebrating the Wrong Things

One of the strangest leadership habits I ever observed in the Navy involved something that sounded like a success.

Commands love metrics.

Days without a safety incident.
Days without a mishap.
Days without a disciplinary event.

At first glance, those numbers feel like evidence that leadership is working.

But sometimes those numbers start measuring the wrong thing.

One of the most common examples was the DUI briefing.

If you've spent any time in the Navy, you've probably heard one.

Usually on a Friday.

Someone stands up in front of the command and announces how many days it has been since the last DUI.

"Command, we are currently at 63 days without a DUI."

Maybe 120.
Sometimes higher.

And every time the number increases, it becomes something people start celebrating.

It gets mentioned in meetings.
It shows up on slides.
Sometimes someone even congratulates the command for maintaining the streak.

But after a while, something about that never sat right with me.

Because a DUI is not a leadership metric.

It's an individual decision.

A sailor choosing to drive after drinking does not happen because a command went 62 days without it.

And it is not prevented simply because leadership is tracking a number on a board.

Yet over time, commands began measuring success by how long it had been since someone made a bad decision.

It was a strange way of framing the issue.

Because when you really think about it, what we were celebrating was the absence of failure.

Not the presence of good judgment.

Those are not the same thing.

And that's when something my Commanding Officer, Justin Banz, once told me really started to make sense.

"We are what we celebrate".

That line stuck with me.

Because if a command celebrates "days without a DUI," then what it is really reinforcing is avoidance.

Don't mess up.

Don't be the one who resets the counter.

That is very different from teaching people how to make better decisions.

Eventually, I started noticing another pattern.

Many sailors believed something that simply wasn't true.

They believed that if they stopped drinking early enough in the evening, they would automatically be safe to drive the next morning.

The logic sounded reasonable.

"CMC, I stopped drinking at midnight."
"CMC, I had plenty of time to sober up."

Most people assumed that after a few hours of sleep, the alcohol would be gone.

But that assumption didn't always match reality. Alcohol doesn't leave the body as quickly as people think.

The body processes alcohol at a steady rate, and depending on how much someone drank, that process can take far longer than expected.

So instead of giving another lecture, we decided to demonstrate the reality.

The Experiment

There was another part of this story that made the experiment more meaningful.

The idea hadn't started at that command.

Years earlier, I had asked multiple commanding officers if we could try something like this.

Six different COs.

Every single one said no.

Not because they disagreed with the goal.

They all supported DUI prevention.

But the response was always the same.

It felt too risky.

What if someone blew a high number?
What if the message was misunderstood?
What if it created the wrong perception?

So the idea never moved forward.

It stayed one of those concepts that sounded good in theory but never actually happened.

Then eventually, I asked another CO.

I explained the idea the same way I always had.

No punishment.
No embarrassment.

Just a controlled demonstration.

Sailors would volunteer, go out on liberty, drink normally, and come in the next morning for a breathalyzer. This was all conducted under leadership supervision the entire time, providing transportation to and from the experiment.

The point wasn't discipline.

It was understanding.

For a moment, I expected the same answer I had always received.

Instead, the CO paused and said something simple.

"Let's do it."

Just like that.

No long debate.

No hesitation.

Just a decision.

And that decision made all the difference.

Because once we ran the experiment, the impact was immediate.

The volunteers came in the next morning confident they would blow zero.

They had stopped drinking hours earlier.
They had slept.
They felt fine.

But when the breathalyzer results appeared, the mood changed.

Several sailors still had alcohol in their system.

Not necessarily enough to get arrested.

But clearly not zero.

Clearly not fully sober.

The reaction was immediate.

"Wow."
"Seriously?"
"I thought I was fine."

But what stood out even more was what one of the sailors said afterward.

"CMC… I've never seen anything like this before."

And he meant it in a good way.

Because for once, the command wasn't just giving another lecture.

We were showing them reality.

The sailors respected that.

They understood that leadership was trying to help them learn, not just reminding them about the rules.

And I remember walking away from that moment thinking something simple.

Sometimes leadership isn't about having the perfect idea.

Sometimes it's about being the person willing to say yes when everyone else has been saying no.

Leadership Lesson

Metrics can be useful tools.

But they can also create misleading signals if leaders are not careful.

When organizations celebrate the absence of failure rather than the presence of good judgment, they reinforce the wrong behavior.

Counting days since the last mistake does not mean people are making better decisions. It only means the mistake hasn't happened recently.

Effective leadership focuses on developing judgment, not protecting statistics.

People make better decisions when they understand the reasoning behind policies and experience the consequences in meaningful ways.

That is why experiential learning works.

Because people remember what they see.

And more importantly, they remember what they feel.

The Corporate Mirror

Corporate organizations face the same challenge with performance metrics.

Companies track numbers to demonstrate progress.

Safety statistics.
Quarterly targets.
Customer satisfaction scores.
Operational metrics.

Each of these begins with a reasonable intention.

But over time, metrics can become something else.

They become something to protect.

And when that happens, behavior changes.

People start prioritizing the number instead of the outcome.

Problems get delayed instead of reported.
Small issues get hidden to protect performance.
Teams focus on appearances instead of reality.

Organizations slowly drift into a culture where success is defined by what gets reported, not what actually exists.

The most effective leaders recognize this early.

They treat metrics as indicators, not trophies.

Numbers should guide conversations.

They should never define success.

Because just like in the Navy, the goal is not to eliminate every mistake.

That is impossible.

The goal is to build an environment where people learn, adjust, and make better decisions over time.

And that kind of growth does not come from celebrating a number on a board.

It comes from understanding what actually drives behavior.

Because in the end, we are what we celebrate.

Chapter 5
The Split Shift

Operational problems rarely announce themselves politely.

They show up slowly.

Workloads increase.
Schedules tighten.
People start working longer hours.

Everyone pushes a little harder to keep things moving.

At first, it just feels like a busy period.

But eventually, the strain becomes visible.

That was the situation we were facing at HSM-51.

The squadron was operating at a high tempo. Aircraft were flying constantly, maintenance demands were increasing, and the same group of sailors were responsible for keeping everything moving.

Like most operational units, the default response was simple.

Work harder.
Stay later.
Push through it.

And for a while, that works.

Sailors are remarkably capable of pushing through long days and heavy workloads. The culture of aviation maintenance encourages exactly that kind of resilience.

But resilience has limits.

Eventually fatigue starts creeping into the system.

People get tired.
Communication becomes less precise.
Small mistakes begin to appear.

None of it looks catastrophic in isolation.

But when leaders are paying attention, those small signals tell a clear story.

The system is under stress.

Around that time, I started thinking about a different approach.

Instead of asking the same group of sailors to stretch their day further and further, what if we split the workload?

Two teams.
Separate shifts.

The idea wasn't complicated.

Instead of one continuous crew carrying the entire workload, the responsibility would rotate between two teams working longer shifts on alternating days. Each team owned the full operational cycle during their shift, then stepped away completely—giving them real recovery time before rotating back in.

In theory, it would reduce fatigue, improve focus, and sustain the operational tempo without burning people out.

But new ideas rarely get immediate support.

Especially when the current system technically works.

When the idea first surfaced, the reaction was cautious.

Splitting the team raised legitimate concerns.

Would communication break down between shifts?
Would accountability become unclear?
Would coordination suffer?

Fair questions.

Any time you change how people work together, new risks appear.

And organizations default to a familiar answer:

If the system isn't broken, why change it?

So the idea lingered.

Discussed.
Considered.
Not implemented.

Until something forced the decision.

Then COVID arrived.

Like it did everywhere else, the pandemic disrupted normal operations almost overnight.

Suddenly, the concerns that had slowed down the split shift idea became less important than a new reality.

The squadron had to operate while minimizing contact between groups.

Separation was no longer a preference.

It was a requirement.

And the split shift model suddenly made perfect sense.

Two teams.
Separate work cycles.
Limited overlap.

The structure that once seemed unnecessary now solved an entirely different problem.

So the squadron implemented the split shift.

And something interesting happened.

Operations didn't slow down.

They improved.

Flight hours increased.
Maintenance continued moving.
Fatigue began to ease.

Two focused teams proved more effective than one exhausted group trying to carry everything at once.

The solution that once felt risky turned out to be exactly what the situation required.

Looking back, the most interesting part of the story isn't that the split shift worked.

It's that the idea existed before the crisis forced the change.

That happens more often than leaders realize.

Organizations frequently contain the seeds of solutions long before they become willing to use them.

Ideas surface.
People talk about them.
But inertia keeps the existing system in place until external pressure forces action.

In this case, the pandemic became that pressure.

And once the shift structure was implemented, the benefits became obvious.

Better focus.
Better pacing.
Sustainable operations.

It reinforced something I had been learning over time.

Good ideas often arrive before people are ready to adopt them.

Sometimes those ideas wait quietly until circumstances create the right moment.

The challenge for leaders is recognizing them when they appear.

Because when the moment comes, the organization won't have time to start from scratch.

It will need those ideas immediately.

Leadership Lesson

Organizations often resist change when the current system still appears to work.

But "working" and "working well" are not the same thing.

Leaders need to pay attention to early signals of strain.

Fatigue.
Inefficiency.
Communication breakdowns.

Those signals usually appear long before failure.

And they are often the clearest indicators that the system needs adjustment.

The strongest leaders act before the system breaks.

Because waiting for failure is rarely a strategy.

It's a reaction.

The Corporate Mirror

After transitioning into the corporate world, I started seeing the same pattern play out in business organizations.

Teams push harder.

Work hours stretch longer.

People absorb increasing workloads because the system technically still functions.

And leaders hesitate to introduce structural change because nothing has completely broken yet.

Instead of redesigning the workload, organizations simply ask people to carry more pressure.

Until eventually something forces a change.

A missed deadline.
A client issue.
A financial shock.
Or a global event like a pandemic.

Then suddenly, the organization becomes willing to adopt ideas that had been discussed months—or even years—earlier.

Remote work is one of the clearest examples.

For years, many companies resisted it. Managers worried about productivity, coordination, and accountability.

Then COVID forced the experiment.

And many organizations discovered that the system could function differently than they had assumed.

The pattern is consistent.

Good ideas often appear early.

But organizations hesitate until circumstances remove the option to wait.

Strong leaders pay attention to those early signals.

Because when conditions change, the best solutions are often already sitting inside the organization.

Waiting.

Chapter 6
Free Chicken

Leadership lessons do not always come from formal training.

Sometimes they come from a single sentence someone says in passing that perfectly captures something leaders deal with every day.

One of those moments happened during my time with HSM-51 Five.

The phrase came from Captain Banz, who was serving as the Commanding Officer.

Like most aviation commands, department head meetings followed a familiar rhythm.

Operations updates.
Maintenance discussions.
Personnel issues.
Planning for upcoming events.

And occasionally, someone would bring forward a question that technically required the commanding officer's approval.

Not because it was a major decision.

But because somewhere along the way, the organization had decided it needed to go higher.

The discussion would start simply.

Someone would explain the situation.
Another person would add context.
Someone else would ask a clarifying question.

And slowly, the conversation would expand into something bigger than it needed to be.

That's when Captain Banz said something that stuck immediately.

"CMC... that's free chicken."

The first time I heard it, I laughed.

Because the phrase perfectly captured what was happening.

The decision was obvious.

There was no real risk.
No meaningful downside.

The answer was already yes.

But the organization had still managed to build a process around it.

And just like that, "free chicken" became shorthand.

If something was free chicken, it meant the decision was easy.
It meant the authority already existed.
It meant there was no reason to overthink it.

Just say yes and move on.

The phrase spread quickly.

Sometimes it came up in meetings.
Sometimes in hallway conversations.
Sometimes someone would stop mid-explanation and realize it themselves.

"Oh… never mind. That's free chicken."

Everyone would laugh.

Decision made.

Move forward.

What made the phrase powerful wasn't just that it was funny.

It was that it exposed something leaders often fail to see.

Decision friction.

Organizations create it constantly.

Policies.
Approval chains.

Extra coordination.
Layers of oversight.

Sometimes those are necessary.

But sometimes they exist simply because no one has stopped to question them.

And over time, those layers start to feel normal.

People begin asking permission for things they already have the authority to do.

They escalate decisions that never needed to move upward.

They add discussion to problems that already have answers.

"Free chicken" cut through all of that.

It reminded everyone in the room that leadership is not just about making decisions.

Sometimes it's about recognizing when the decision is already made.

And having the discipline to not complicate it.

How It Spread

What surprised me most was how quickly the phrase became part of the culture.

Within weeks, people across the command were using it.

Junior officers.
Department heads.
Chiefs.

It became a shared signal.

A way to recognize something simple but important:

Not every decision is hard.

Leaders are trained to look for risk.

Risk management.
Risk mitigation.
Risk avoidance.

Those things matter.

But when leaders only focus on risk, they start missing something else.

Opportunity.

Low-risk decisions.
Clear yes answers.
Small approvals that unlock progress.

Those are the moments that keep organizations moving.

And those are the moments people hesitate on the most.

Because once you're in charge, something subtle happens.

People start asking you for permission.

Even when they don't need it.

Sometimes they want reassurance.
Sometimes they want confirmation.
Sometimes they just don't want to be wrong.

And if leaders are not careful, that dynamic slowly reshapes the organization.

Everything starts moving upward.

Everything starts waiting.

And over time, people stop exercising judgment.

That's the real cost.

Not delay.

Dependence.

Recognizing free chicken decisions breaks that cycle.

It reminds people that not everything requires approval.

Not everything requires analysis.

And not everything requires leadership involvement.

Sometimes the answer is already yes.

Leadership Lesson

One of the core responsibilities of leadership is knowing where to apply effort—and where to remove it.

Some problems require deep analysis.

Some require fast action.

But many decisions fall into a third category.

They are already decided.

Leaders who fail to recognize that create unnecessary friction.

When every decision is treated as complex, organizations slow down.

People stop acting.
They start waiting.
Small decisions climb the chain.

Initiative drops.

Confidence drops.

And the organization becomes less effective than it should be.

The best leaders do something different.

They recognize when something is already clear.

They remove barriers.

They trust people.

They keep things moving.

They recognize the free chicken.

The Corporate Mirror

Corporate organizations struggle with this even more.

In many environments, approval structures are designed to manage risk.

Multiple layers of management.
Formal review processes.
Cross-functional coordination.
Legal review.
Budget approval.
Executive oversight.

Each step makes sense on its own.

But together, they can create massive friction around small decisions.

Employees learn quickly:

It's safer to ask than to act.

And that changes behavior.

Projects slow down.
Innovation slows down.
Simple opportunities get missed.

Not because people don't see them.

Because no one wants to be the one who just said yes.

The result is familiar.

Meetings about decisions that should take thirty seconds.

Email chains discussing things that were already obvious.

Requests for approval that were never actually required.

The best organizations actively fight this.

They push authority down.

They encourage initiative.

They reward good judgment instead of punishing small mistakes.

Because they understand something simple.

Speed matters.

And speed doesn't come from more process.

It comes from removing unnecessary decisions.

Because in the end, some choices are complicated.

Some carry risk.

Some require real leadership.

And some…

Are already decided.

Those are the moments when a leader doesn't need another meeting.

Doesn't need another slide.

Doesn't need another opinion.

They just need to recognize it.

Smile.

And say it.

"That's free chicken."

Chapter 7
SIAP — Self-Induced Ass Pain

Some of the best leadership lessons I learned didn't come from formal training.

They came from moments when someone said something so simple—and so accurate—that it instantly explained problems I had been seeing for years but didn't yet have the language to describe.

One of those moments happened during my time with Carrier Air Wing Five.

Like most operational commands, department head meetings covered everything.

Operations updates.
Maintenance timelines.
Personnel challenges.
Safety concerns.
Logistics issues.

The agenda was always full, and every department had its own priorities competing for attention.

The job of the leadership team was to sort through all of it and keep the organization moving.

During one particular meeting, the conversation started drifting into a pattern that will be familiar to anyone who has worked inside a large organization.

A relatively small problem had come up.

But like many organizational problems, it had already started growing—because of the number of policies and processes wrapped around it.

People began offering solutions.

New procedures.
Additional steps.
Extra reporting requirements.

Someone suggested another review layer.

Another proposed a checklist to make sure it never happened again.

Individually, every suggestion made sense.

No one was trying to make things harder.

Everyone was trying to prevent the problem from coming back.

But the conversation kept expanding.

More controls.
More oversight.
More process.

At some point, we had stopped solving the problem and started building a system around it.

That's when Mike Feldhues spoke up.

Mike was the Carrier Air Wing Five CAGMO at the time. Like a lot of strong leaders, he had a habit of listening quietly—and then saying something that reset the entire room.

He leaned forward and said:

"This sounds like SIAP."

A few people looked up.

Someone asked what he meant.

Mike didn't miss a beat.

"Self-Induced Ass Pain."

The room laughed.

Like a lot of moments in military meetings, the humor broke the tension just enough to reset the conversation.

Then we moved on.

Next agenda item.
Operations.
Maintenance.
Personnel.

But the phrase stuck with me.

After the meeting, I caught Mike in the passageway.

"Hey—what exactly did you mean by that?"

He smiled, like he'd been waiting for the question.

"SIAP," he said again. "Self-Induced Ass Pain."

Then he explained it in a way that stayed with me for the rest of my career. Organizations spend a lot of time dealing with problems they created themselves.

Not because people are incompetent.

Not because leaders are trying to make things harder.

But because over time, we keep adding layers.

Policies. Approvals. Extra steps.

Every time something goes wrong, the instinct is to add another control.

Another rule. Another form. Another briefing.

Individually, those changes make sense.

Collectively, they create friction.

Eventually, the system becomes so complicated that the organization starts slowing itself down.

At that point, the problem isn't the mission anymore.

The problem is the system.

"That's SIAP," he said.

Self-Induced Ass Pain.

The more I thought about it, the more I started seeing it everywhere.

Organizations accumulate processes over time.

Rules.
Checklists.
Approvals.
Forms.

Some of those are necessary—especially in environments like aviation, where discipline and procedure directly impact safety.

But over time, organizations often forget why those systems were created in the first place.

Processes expand.

New rules get layered on top of old ones.

Additional steps get added because someone, somewhere, experienced a problem leadership wanted to prevent from ever happening again.

Eventually, the system starts creating the very friction it was meant to eliminate.

That's SIAP in action.

And the painful part is how quietly it develops.

No single decision causes it.

No leader wakes up and decides to create bureaucracy.

It builds gradually.

One rule at a time.
One approval at a time.
One extra step at a time.

Until people spend more time navigating the system than accomplishing the mission.

Once I started recognizing the pattern, I couldn't stop seeing it.

Simple tasks requiring multiple signatures.

Minor issues triggering long reporting chains.

Straightforward decisions delayed because no one wanted to be the one who approved them.

Every step had a justification.

Every layer had a story.

But together, they created drag.

And the organization slowed itself down.

The irony is that organizations rarely recognize when they've crossed that line.

From the inside, every rule still feels justified.

Every process still appears necessary.

It's only when someone steps back and asks a simple question that the problem becomes clear:

Are we solving the mission…
Or managing the system?

That question cuts straight to the heart of SIAP.

Because organizations suffering from self-induced friction often become very good at maintaining systems—and very slow at producing results.

The system becomes the focus.

Not the mission.

And when that happens, behavior changes.

People stop asking how to solve problems.

They start asking how to avoid triggering more process.

They stop taking initiative.

They start waiting for approval.

They stop thinking creatively.

They follow the safest path through the system.

The organization becomes slower.

Less adaptable.

Less confident.

All because of systems it built itself.

One of the reasons SIAP stuck with me is that it gave leaders permission to question things that had quietly become normal.

Sometimes the best leadership decision isn't creating a new rule.

Sometimes it's removing one.

Eliminating friction.

Simplifying the process.

Returning to the original purpose.

That doesn't mean lowering standards.

It doesn't mean ignoring safety.

It means recognizing when systems have grown beyond their intent.

Good leaders maintain discipline.

Great leaders maintain clarity.

They constantly evaluate whether the systems around them are helping the mission—or slowing it down.

And when leaders are willing to ask that question honestly, something changes.

People start focusing on outcomes again.

Instead of managing the system, they start solving problems.

Instead of protecting the process, they start protecting the mission.

That shift changes culture.

Because once people recognize unnecessary friction, they begin challenging it.

They identify where work can move faster.

They question policies that no longer serve a purpose.

And gradually, the organization becomes more agile.

More responsive.

More effective.

That's the power of recognizing SIAP.

It reminds leaders that not every problem requires more structure.

Sometimes the real solution is less.

Leadership Lesson

Organizations naturally accumulate processes over time.

Most of those systems are created with good intentions.

But when leaders stop evaluating whether those systems still serve their purpose, they quickly become obstacles.

Strong leaders recognize when friction has become self-inflicted.

They simplify.

They remove what is no longer necessary.

They restore focus on the mission instead of the system.

Because complexity grows on its own.

Clarity requires leadership.

The Corporate Mirror

When I transitioned into the corporate world, I realized quickly that SIAP isn't unique to the military.

If anything, it's more common.

Corporate systems follow the same pattern.

A problem occurs.

A policy is created to prevent it.

Another issue appears somewhere else.

Another rule is added.

Another approval layer.

Another reporting requirement.

Over time, employees find themselves navigating multiple layers just to complete basic tasks.

Budgets require multiple sign-offs.

Routine decisions require meetings.

Projects slow down while people wait for consensus.

And just like in the military, every step seems reasonable on its own.

But together, they create friction.

Momentum disappears.

Instead of focusing on results, people focus on compliance.

Instead of solving problems, they follow process.

The organization becomes safe.

Predictable.

And slow.

That's corporate SIAP.

Self-Induced Ass Pain.

The companies that succeed understand something simple:

Speed matters.

Adaptability matters.

And unnecessary complexity quietly kills both.

Strong leaders recognize when systems begin choking initiative.

They ask the same question:

Are we solving the mission…
Or managing the system?

And then they act.

They remove layers.

They streamline decisions.

They push authority closer to the work.

Because whether you're running an air wing or a global company, the principle is the same.

Complexity grows naturally.

Simplicity requires leadership.

And sometimes the most effective decision a leader can make…

Is removing a rule.

Chapter 8
When Leaders Optimize for Themselves

Leadership decisions are rarely made in isolation.

They exist inside systems.
Inside cultures.
Inside organizations where people are constantly balancing risk, responsibility, and reputation.

Most leaders like to believe their decisions are guided by one thing above all else:

The mission.

But the longer you spend inside organizations—military or corporate—the more you start noticing something uncomfortable.

Not every decision is made for the mission.

Sometimes decisions are made to protect the leader.

That realization took time for me to fully understand.

Early in my career, I assumed that every rule, every policy, and every restriction had been created for good reasons. I believed that leadership systems were designed to maximize effectiveness and protect people.

In many cases, that assumption was true.

But not always.

Over time, I began to notice that some policies didn't really make the mission stronger. They didn't necessarily make the organization safer. They didn't improve performance.

What they often did was reduce risk for the person making the decision.

Those policies weren't built around mission success.

They were built around career protection.

And once you start seeing that pattern, you notice it everywhere.

One of the clearest examples involved liberty policies.

Liberty is a simple concept in the military. When sailors aren't on duty, they are free to go out, relax, spend time with friends, and decompress.

That matters.

Operational environments are stressful, and people need time away from the job.

But liberty policies have a way of becoming increasingly restrictive over time. Often after a single incident.

A DUI.
A fight downtown.
Someone making a bad decision after a few drinks.

When something like that happens, leadership feels pressure to respond. There is always a sense that if something went wrong, the system must need tightening.

So a new rule gets created.

Maybe sailors now have to move in groups.
Maybe they need a designated non-drinker.
Maybe they have to submit a liberty plan.
Maybe curfews get adjusted.

Each new rule arrives with the same logic:

Prevent the next problem.
Protect the command.
Reduce risk.

But the problem with those policies is that they often ignore a basic truth.

People make individual decisions.

And no amount of group policy eliminates personal responsibility.

At one command, I remember a policy that required sailors to go out in groups of four if alcohol was involved.

One person in the group had to remain sober.

On paper, the rule sounded logical.

A built-in safety mechanism. Someone responsible for getting the group home safely.

But the policy ran into reality almost immediately.

Sailors didn't necessarily want to go out in groups of four.

They didn't always want someone in the group staying sober all night.

And more importantly, the rule pushed sailors toward compliance instead of judgment.

Instead of thinking about personal responsibility, people started thinking about how to technically satisfy the policy.

Find a fourth person.
Designate the sober one.
Submit the plan.
Check the boxes.

Once the boxes were checked, the system considered the risk managed.

But the reality was obvious.

People still made their own decisions.

The rule didn't eliminate bad judgment.

It simply created the appearance that leadership had addressed the issue.

And that is where the idea of leaders optimizing for themselves begins to show up.

When a rule like that is implemented, leadership can point to the policy and say they took action.

If another incident occurs, the command can show that controls were in place.

In other words, the policy protects the leader.

It demonstrates that leadership responded.
That risk was managed.
That procedures were implemented.

But the mission—or in this case, the behavior of individuals—doesn't necessarily improve.

The policy exists primarily as protection.

There was another problem with policies like that, and it became obvious the moment you applied the rule across an entire command.

At the time, I was the Command Master Chief.

An E-9.

The senior enlisted advisor to the commanding officer.

Now imagine applying that same liberty rule to everyone equally.

Four people.
One non-drinker.
A liberty plan.

Technically, it applied to me too.

Which meant that if I wanted to go out to dinner with someone, I would need to bring three sailors along.

That's when the absurdity becomes obvious.

Because I'm not taking sailors on dates.

That's not how leadership works.

And yet on paper, the policy treated everyone exactly the same.

Which meant the rule was clearly written for appearance rather than reality.

It was designed to demonstrate that leadership had implemented controls.

It wasn't designed around how people actually live.

When policies reach that point—when they clearly don't apply to the people responsible for enforcing them—it usually means something deeper is happening.

The rule isn't really about behavior.

It's about protection.

Protection for leadership.

If something goes wrong, the command can point to the policy.

They can say the system was in place.
That guidance existed.
That expectations were clearly communicated.

But the people living inside that system immediately recognize the gap between policy and reality.

And once people start seeing that gap, trust begins to erode.

Not because leaders intended to create unfair rules.

But because the rules reveal something uncomfortable.

The system wasn't built entirely for the mission.

It was built, at least in part, to protect the people running it.

And once I started noticing that dynamic, I began seeing it everywhere.

Rules designed not to improve outcomes, but to prove that leadership had "done something."

Most leaders aren't sitting in meetings thinking about how to protect their careers.

But organizations naturally drift toward systems that reduce personal accountability for leaders.

More approvals.
More policies.
More oversight layers.

Each new rule reduces decision risk for the person at the top.

But it also slows the organization.

And sometimes it weakens trust.

Because people inside organizations are not blind.

They can tell the difference between a rule designed to help them and a rule designed to protect leadership.

When people believe rules exist to protect the mission, they follow them with discipline.

When they believe rules exist to protect leadership, they comply—but often without respect.

That difference matters.

Leadership credibility is built on trust.

And trust erodes quickly when people believe leaders are more concerned about protecting themselves than empowering the team.

The irony is that most leaders don't realize when they've crossed that line.

They see themselves as responsible decision-makers.

They see policies as necessary safeguards.

But if those policies consistently shift responsibility away from individuals and toward systems, the organization becomes more rigid.

More cautious.
Less adaptable.
Less capable of moving quickly.

That's when initiative begins to disappear.

People stop making decisions.

They wait for guidance.

They avoid risk.

They become careful rather than effective.

And slowly, the organization loses one of its most valuable qualities.

Momentum.

Because momentum requires trust.

Trust that individuals will act responsibly.
Trust that leaders will support reasonable decisions.
Trust that the mission—not personal protection—is the real priority.

When leaders optimize primarily for their own protection, that trust weakens. And once trust weakens, every system inside the organization becomes heavier.

More approvals.
More oversight.
More control.
More friction.

Leadership requires accepting risk.

Not reckless risk.

But the risk that comes from trusting people to operate with judgment.

When leaders try to eliminate all risk, they inevitably create systems that restrict initiative.

And those systems rarely produce better outcomes.

They produce slower ones.

Leadership Lesson

Strong leadership requires accepting that not every decision can be protected by policy.

When leaders prioritize protecting themselves over empowering their teams, organizations become rigid and slow.

Leaders who focus on mission success instead of personal protection build cultures where initiative, trust, and accountability can thrive.

Because leadership is not about avoiding responsibility. It is about carrying it.

The Corporate Mirror

When I transitioned into the corporate world, I quickly realized this pattern exists far beyond military organizations. Corporate environments struggle with the same leadership dynamic.

Executives are responsible for results.
They are accountable to boards, investors, and stakeholders.

And when something goes wrong, the pressure to demonstrate control is immediate.

Just like in the military, the instinctive response is often to add process.

More approvals.
More documentation.
More oversight.

A single incident can trigger new compliance structures across the entire organization.

On paper, those changes are designed to reduce risk.

In reality, they often shift risk away from leadership and onto the system.

A decision that once required one person's judgment now requires five signatures.

A project that once moved quickly now requires multiple reviews.

A simple idea now needs approval from multiple departments.

Each step reduces personal exposure for the leader.

But collectively, those steps slow everything down.

Employees stop focusing on results and start focusing on navigation.

How do I get this approved?
Who needs to sign off?
What process protects me if this goes wrong?

That is how initiative dies.

Innovation slows.
Momentum disappears.
People start optimizing for safety instead of effectiveness.

And just like in military organizations, the companies that remain competitive are the ones that understand something simple:

Speed matters.

Trust matters.

And systems designed primarily to protect leadership eventually choke both.

The strongest leaders recognize when their organizations are drifting toward self-protection instead of mission success.

They simplify.

They empower.

They remove unnecessary approval layers.

They accept that leadership sometimes requires making decisions without perfect insulation.

Because ultimately, leadership is not about eliminating risk.

It is about accepting responsibility.

And the organizations that thrive are usually led by people willing to carry that responsibility themselves—

Instead of building systems designed to avoid it.

Chapter 9
When the Armor Stops Working

There is a moment in most leadership careers when something quietly changes.

It doesn't happen during a ceremony.
It doesn't happen when a promotion is announced.
And it doesn't come with any warning.

But at some point, leaders begin to realize that the authority they once relied on no longer carries the same weight.

Early in a career, authority is simple.

Rank speaks clearly.
Orders are followed.
Positions come with built-in respect.

When you're junior, the structure of the organization does a lot of the work for you.

The uniform matters.
The title matters.
The position matters.

But over time, something begins to shift.

The higher someone climbs, the less those things matter on their own.

At some point, people are no longer responding primarily to rank.

They are responding to credibility.

That transition is subtle. But it's one of the most important realizations a leader can have.

Early in my career, I admired senior leaders the same way many young sailors do.

Chiefs.
Senior Chiefs.
Master Chiefs.
The khakis.

Those uniforms carried authority.

When a Chief spoke, people listened.

When a Master Chief walked into a room, the atmosphere changed.

At least that's how it appeared from the outside.

The assumption was simple:

They had earned that authority through experience and competence.

And many of them had.

But over time—especially once I stepped into senior enlisted roles myself—I started seeing something that younger sailors don't always notice.

Not all authority is equal.

Some leaders rely on the uniform.

Others rely on trust.

And those are not the same thing.

The uniform gives someone the ability to give orders.

Trust gives someone the ability to influence people—even when they don't have to listen.

That difference becomes critical at the senior levels of leadership.

Because eventually…

Rank stops doing the work.

When someone becomes a Command Master Chief, a commanding officer, or a senior executive, the people around them already understand the structure.

They know who is in charge.

But what determines how effective that leader becomes isn't the title.

It's credibility.

That's when the armor starts coming off.

Earlier in a career, rank acts like armor.

It protects leaders from resistance.
It shields them from criticism.
It creates automatic compliance.

But at the senior level, that armor doesn't function the same way.

The people around you are no longer junior.

They're experienced professionals.

Department heads.
Senior managers.
Executives.

People who have spent years inside the system.

They're not impressed by titles.

They're evaluating something else.

Judgment.
Consistency.
Integrity.

And they form those judgments quickly. Once that happens, something subtle begins to change. People still follow the leader. But the energy behind that compliance shifts. If the leader has credibility, the team leans forward.

People speak up. They offer ideas. They take initiative. They solve problems early.

But if credibility is missing, the opposite happens.

People comply.

But they don't commit.

They follow instructions.

But they hold back their best thinking.

They avoid initiative.

They protect themselves.

The system still functions.

But the organization loses something critical.

Momentum.

I saw this dynamic play out many times.

Some leaders walked into a room and immediately elevated the conversation. People trusted their judgment. They listened carefully. They knew decisions would be grounded in the mission and the people involved. Other leaders had the same rank.

The same position.

The same authority.

But the room felt completely different.

Conversations became cautious.

Ideas were withheld.

People waited to see which way the leader leaned before speaking.

Not because those leaders were bad people.

But because trust hadn't been built.

That's when the realization hits.

Rank might get you into the room. But credibility determines what happens once you're there. This can be uncomfortable. Especially for leaders who spent years relying on positional authority.

Because positional authority is simple.

Credibility is not.

Credibility is earned daily.

Through decisions.
Through consistency.
Through how leaders treat people.
Through whether actions match words.

When credibility is strong, leaders rarely need to remind anyone of their authority. The team recognizes it naturally. When credibility is weak, leaders often fall back on the only tool they believe they have left.

The title.

The hierarchy.

The position.

But that approach rarely works for long.

Because once people begin to see a leader relying on authority instead of judgment, the organization adjusts.

People follow the structure.

But trust never fully develops.

And without trust, performance plateaus.

One of the hardest lessons in leadership is this:

Credibility cannot be demanded.

It cannot be assigned.

It cannot be ordered.

It has to be earned.

And it has to be maintained.

Every decision either strengthens it or weakens it.

Every interaction either builds trust or erodes it.

That responsibility never goes away.

In fact, the higher someone rises, the more important credibility becomes.

Because at the top, there are fewer layers of structure supporting the leader.

The system assumes they already understand the responsibility.

Which means the armor provides less protection.

And the weight of leadership becomes more visible.

That's when the truth becomes clear.

Authority may place you in the role.

But credibility determines whether people truly follow.

Leadership Lesson

Authority can require compliance.

Credibility inspires commitment.

The most effective leaders understand that positional power fades.

What remains is the trust they build through judgment, integrity, and consistency.

When credibility is strong, teams move faster.

They think more clearly.

They act with confidence.

When credibility is weak, organizations become cautious, slow, and risk-averse.

Because leadership is not sustained by authority.

It is sustained by trust.

The Corporate Mirror

When I moved into the corporate world, I saw the same dynamic immediately.

Corporate organizations also operate within hierarchies.

Titles.
Reporting structures.
Executive authority.

But just like in the military, the higher someone climbs, the less the title alone guarantees influence.

Executives sit in rooms with other executives.

Managers work alongside experienced professionals.

And just like before, people form judgments quickly.

Not based on a title.

But based on behavior.

Judgment.
Consistency.
Integrity.

Leaders who demonstrate those qualities build credibility.

Their teams trust them.

They move faster.

They operate with confidence.

But leaders who rely primarily on authority run into the same problem.

People comply.

But they don't commit.

Ideas slow down.

Initiative declines.

The organization becomes cautious.

And momentum fades.

The strongest leaders understand something simple.

Credibility is built through behavior.

Every decision sends a signal.

Every action reinforces—or weakens—the trust people place in leadership.

And once that trust exists, organizations operate differently.

Faster.
More confidently.
More collaboratively.

That's when leadership stops relying on authority.

And starts relying on something far more powerful.

Belief.

Chapter 10
The Meeting After the Meeting

Anyone who has spent time inside a large organization knows that meetings rarely end when the meeting actually ends.

The agenda wraps up.
The slides are finished.
The leader says, "Alright, that's all we have today."

People gather their notebooks.

Chairs slide back.

And conversations begin as everyone heads toward the door.

Then something interesting happens.

The real meeting starts.

In the hallway.
In the parking lot.
Walking back to the office.

Sometimes it happens between two people who linger behind after everyone else leaves.

It's so common that experienced leaders recognize it immediately.

The formal discussion ends.

But the most honest conversation begins afterward.

In the Navy, this dynamic showed up constantly.

Department head meetings.
Wardroom discussions.
Command briefings.

No matter how structured the meeting was, the same pattern repeated. Inside the room, people spoke carefully. They presented updates, explained their positions and asked questions within the boundaries of the discussion.

But once the meeting ended and people stepped outside, the tone shifted.

"Did that make sense to you?"

"I'm not sure we're solving the right problem."

"There's more going on here than what we just talked about."

Those conversations weren't disloyal.

They were honest.

Inside formal meetings, people operate within structure.

Rank matters.
Time matters.
Perception matters.

But once that structure disappears, people relax.

They speak more directly.

And that's when leaders can learn what the organization is actually thinking.

As a senior enlisted leader, I started paying close attention to those moments. Not because I was looking for complaints. But because those conversations often revealed what hadn't surfaced inside the room. Sometimes the meeting had addressed the wrong problem. Sometimes the proposed solution created new concerns. Sometimes people just needed space to process what they had heard.

That space is where clarity shows up.

The conversation after the meeting is often where the real understanding begins.

And that's where leaders should be listening.

Good leaders don't ignore that moment. They use it, because it tells you something important:

Did the team actually understand—and support—the direction that was just set?

If the hallway conversations reflect clarity, that's a good sign.

If they reveal confusion or hesitation, something was missed.

One of the challenges with formal meetings is that they often create a kind of performance environment. People are aware of who is in the room. They are aware of rank, personalities, and time pressure. So discussions tend to stay within safe boundaries. That doesn't mean people are being dishonest. It means they are operating within the structure. But once that structure drops, the conversation becomes more candid.

And candid conversations are where leaders get the truth.

Over time, I realized something else. If the real conversation is consistently happening after the meeting, then something is wrong with the meeting. Either people don't feel comfortable speaking openly...

Or the environment doesn't encourage it. That's a leadership problem. Because the purpose of a meeting isn't to complete an agenda. It's to make good decisions. And good decisions require honest input. If people only feel safe sharing that input after the meeting ends, the leader is operating with incomplete information.

That realization changed how I approached meetings. I stopped treating those hallway conversations as separate. I started treating them as a continuation of the decision process. Sometimes I would walk with people after a meeting and ask simple questions.

"Does that plan make sense?"

"Are we missing something?"

Not confrontational. Just curiosity. And the answers were almost always valuable. Not because people were criticizing leadership. But because they were thinking through the reality of the decision. Those conversations often revealed second-order effects. Things that hadn't been obvious in the room. Things that could be addressed early—before they became problems.

Another lesson from these moments is that disagreement isn't a threat.

It's a requirement.

Healthy organizations don't avoid friction. They use it. If people feel comfortable offering different perspectives, decisions improve. But when disagreement disappears from meetings, it usually means one of two things. Either the team is perfectly aligned...

Or people have decided it's safer to stay quiet.

And if people are quiet inside the room but vocal outside of it, that's a signal.

The environment needs to change.

Strong leaders create space for honest conversation before the meeting ends.

They ask questions, they invite opposing views, they make it clear that thoughtful disagreement is not only acceptable—it's expected. And when leaders do that consistently, something interesting happens. The meeting after the meeting gets shorter. Because the real conversation already happened. In the room.

That's when meetings become effective. Not because everyone agrees. But because everyone was heard. Because the concerns were surfaced. Because the decision was made with full understanding. The meeting ends.

And the team moves forward together.

Leadership Lesson

Meetings only work if they surface the information leaders need to make good decisions.

If the real conversation happens after the meeting ends, something important is being missed.

Strong leaders create environments where people feel comfortable speaking honestly before the discussion concludes.

When teams trust that their input is valued, decisions improve.

And alignment becomes real—not assumed.

The Corporate Mirror

The same dynamic exists in corporate environments.

Anyone who has worked inside a large company has seen it.

The meeting ends.
The presentation wraps up.
Everyone nods.

Then the real conversation begins.

People question the strategy.

They wonder if the timeline is realistic.

Someone admits they don't fully understand what was just decided.

Just like in the military, these conversations aren't resistance.

They're processing.

But they also reveal whether the meeting actually achieved its goal.

Alignment.

The best leaders understand this and work to close the gap.

They ask better questions. They invite honest feedback. They encourage disagreement before decisions are locked in.

Because when people speak openly, organizations move faster.

Problems surface earlier.

Solutions improve.

And the conversations that happen afterward shift.

From confusion…

To execution.

Ultimately, the purpose of a meeting isn't to finish an agenda.

It's to ensure the team leaves the room with clarity.

Clarity on the mission.

Clarity on the decision.

Clarity on what comes next.

When that happens, the meeting after the meeting becomes something much simpler.

A conversation about getting the job done.

Chapter 11
The Corporate Mirror

When I left the Navy after thirty years of service, I expected a lot to change.

The uniform would be gone.
The rank structure would be different.
The culture would feel unfamiliar.

All of that was true.

What I didn't expect was how familiar leadership problems would still feel.

When people talk about transitioning from the military to the corporate world, they often describe the two environments as completely different.

Different missions.
Different language.
Different incentives.
Different systems.

And on the surface, that's accurate.

But once you look past those differences, something becomes obvious. The leadership challenges are almost identical.

Organizations are organizations.

People are people.

And the same dynamics that shape military leadership show up in corporate environments too.

The only thing that really changes, is the vocabulary.

In the military, leaders talk about mission readiness, operational timelines, and command responsibility.

In the corporate world, leaders talk about strategy, deliverables, and alignment.

But underneath those words, the challenges are the same.

Communication.
Decision-making.
Trust.
Accountability.
Momentum.

Those don't change when the uniform comes off.

The first time I sat in corporate meetings, I noticed something immediately. People were spending a lot of time discussing slides.

PowerPoint had become the center of the conversation.

Charts.
Graphs.
Forecasts.
Updates.

Every slide represented progress. Or at least the appearance of progress. But as the discussions continued, something felt off. The conversations weren't always about decisions. They were about presentation.

How the information looked.
How the message landed.
Whether the slide told the right story.

And I had seen that before.

In the Navy, the same thing happened during operational briefings.

Leaders would spend more time refining the briefing than solving the problem. Slides became polished. Language became precise.

But the real question—what decision needs to be made—sometimes stayed unclear. The briefing looked good. But the outcome didn't always change.

The same pattern showed up in corporate meetings. Information was presented. People nodded. The meeting moved on. And then—just like in the Navy—the real conversation started afterward.

"Are we actually doing that?"
"What's the real priority?"
"Does that timeline even make sense?"

That's when it clicked.

The meeting had communicated information.

But it hadn't created alignment.

That's the corporate mirror. The same leadership patterns showing up in a different environment. Because those patterns aren't about the military. They're about people.

People respond to incentives.

They respond to pressure.

They respond to the systems leaders build around them.

If the system rewards presentation, people focus on presentation.

If it rewards compliance, people focus on compliance.

If it rewards results, people focus on results.

Leaders shape those systems—whether they realize it or not.

That's why the transition felt both unfamiliar and completely recognizable at the same time. The terminology changed. The mission changed. But the leadership dynamics didn't.

One of the biggest lessons I carried from the Navy into the corporate world was the importance of clarity. In operational environments, confusion has consequences. A misunderstood instruction can delay a mission. A poorly communicated plan can create risk. Because of that, military organizations emphasize clear intent. Not just what to do. But why it matters.

Corporate environments don't always maintain that same level of clarity. Strategies get announced. Initiatives get launched. But the connection between those actions and the real objective isn't always obvious. People attend meetings. They review presentations. They hear updates. And still leave the room unsure of what actually matters most.

That uncertainty slows everything down. Because when people don't fully understand the objective, they start protecting themselves. They hesitate. They wait. They stay inside the system instead of moving the mission forward. And just like in the military, that behavior kills initiative.

The same pattern shows up in how organizations handle risk.

When something goes wrong, leaders feel pressure to demonstrate control.

And the response is almost always the same.

Add process.
Add oversight.
Add reporting.

Those systems are meant to reduce risk. But they also reduce speed. And speed matters. In both operational and corporate environments, the organizations that move faster usually win.

They adapt quicker.

They solve problems earlier.

They take advantage of opportunities before others even recognize them.

But speed requires something most systems struggle to maintain.

Trust.

Trust that people will make good decisions.

Trust that leaders will support those decisions.

Trust that the mission matters more than individual protection.

That's where the mirror becomes clear.

The principles that create effective military teams are the same ones that create effective business teams.

Clarity.
Trust.
Accountability.
Decisiveness.

Leaders who build those consistently get the same results—no matter the environment.

Teams move faster.

People take initiative.

Problems surface earlier.

Solutions improve.

One of the most surprising realizations for me was how much military leadership experience translates directly into business.

Not because the missions are the same.

But because the foundation is.

People working together toward a shared objective.

When leaders create environments where people understand the mission, trust leadership, and feel empowered to contribute, performance improves.

Uniform or suit—it doesn't matter.

That's the real lesson.

The environment changes.

The language changes.

But leadership doesn't.

Leadership Lesson

Leadership principles travel.

Clarity, trust, accountability, and decisiveness create effective teams in any environment.

The mission may change. The structure may change.

But the fundamentals remain the same.

Leaders who focus on those fundamentals build organizations that move faster, think better, and perform at a higher level—regardless of where they operate.

The Corporate Mirror

One of the most valuable perspectives a leader can develop is the ability to step outside their own system.

Military leaders entering the corporate world often see things others have stopped questioning.

Processes that have grown too complex.

Meetings focused on presentation instead of decisions.

Approval systems that slow momentum.

And the reverse is true as well.

Corporate leaders looking at military organizations often recognize the power of clarity and decisive leadership.

Both environments have strengths.

Both have blind spots.

The advantage belongs to leaders who can see both.

Because once you understand the underlying principles, you stop leading inside a single system.

You start leading across systems.

Military and corporate.

Operational and commercial.

Strategy and execution.

And at that point, the environment becomes secondary.

Because leadership isn't defined by where you are.

It's defined by how you lead.

Chapter 12
The Leader Everyone Thinks They Are

Most leaders believe they are doing a good job.

That isn't arrogance.

It's human nature.

People rarely see themselves as the problem inside a system. They see themselves as the ones trying to make it work.

They believe they are communicating clearly.
They believe they are making fair decisions.
They believe they are supporting their teams.

And in many cases, they genuinely are.

But leadership has a blind spot that almost every leader encounters at some point.

The way leaders see themselves is often very different from the way their teams experience them.

That gap can be small.

Or it can be enormous.

And the size of that gap often determines whether a leader becomes truly effective—or simply holds the position.

Early in my career, I assumed that if a leader had reached a certain rank or position, they must be good at leadership. That assumption makes sense when you're junior.

Promotion looks like validation.

Experience looks like wisdom.

But over time, I realized something important. Advancement and effectiveness are not always the same thing. Some leaders rise because they are strong decision-makers. Some because they understand people. Some because they consistently deliver results. But others rise because they understand the system. They learn how to navigate promotion boards. They learn how to present themselves. They learn how to hit the metrics the organization values. Those skills can build a successful career. But they don't always build an effective leader. Because leadership isn't judged by resumes. It's judged by experience. The experience of the people being led.

Sailors.

Employees.

Teams.

They are always watching. They notice how decisions are made. They notice who gets credit—and who doesn't. They notice who takes responsibility when things go wrong. They notice which leaders listen… and which ones wait for their turn to speak. Over time, those observations form a reputation.

Not the official one.

The real one.

The one people share in quiet conversations.

And that reputation is often very different from the leader's self-image.

One of the most important lessons I learned as a senior enlisted leader was this:

Leaders need feedback more than they realize. Not the formal feedback in evaluations. The honest feedback that rarely shows up on paper. The kind people only share when they trust there won't be consequences. Without that, leaders operate inside an echo chamber. They hear what people think they want to hear. They see the version of the organization the system presents to them. But they don't see the day-to-day reality.

That gap grows over time. Authority increases. Schedules fill with higher-level meetings. Leaders spend less time with the people doing the work. And gradually, their understanding becomes filtered. Information moves upward through layers. Each layer adjusts the message slightly. By the time it reaches the top, it's often incomplete. Or softened. Or shaped to match what people think leadership wants to hear. Not because people are trying to mislead. Because that's how organizations work.

People avoid creating problems.

They avoid appearing negative.

They avoid bringing issues that might reflect poorly on their team.

So the message becomes safer as it travels upward.

Meanwhile, the leader believes everything is functioning well. That's the illusion. The leader sees one version of the organization. The team experiences another. And the longer that gap exists, the harder it becomes to close. Because the leader's confidence continues to grow—while the team's experience slowly drifts away.

Eventually, the difference starts to show. Not through a major failure. Through small signals.

Energy drops.

Initiative fades.

People do exactly what's required—no more, no less.

From the leader's perspective, it can look like a motivation problem. From the team's perspective, it's often a trust problem.

Trust that their input matters.

Trust that concerns will be heard.

Trust that leadership understands what's really happening.

One of the most valuable habits a leader can develop is this:

Regularly testing their own assumptions.

Instead of asking:

"Do I think I'm leading well?"

Ask something harder:

"How does my team experience my leadership?"

That question requires humility.

It requires curiosity.

And sometimes, it requires hearing things that are uncomfortable.

But leaders who ask that question gain something most leaders never fully develop. Perspective. They begin to see the organization from more than one angle. They recognize the difference between intention and impact. And once they see that difference, they can adjust.

That's where real leadership growth happens.

Because leadership isn't static.

It's a continuous process of learning.

Learning how decisions affect people.

Learning how communication shapes behavior.

Learning how systems influence culture.

Leaders who embrace that process keep improving.

Leaders who assume they already understand it eventually stop growing.

And when leaders stop growing…

Their teams notice.

That's why humility matters. Not the kind that avoids responsibility. The kind that stays curious. Curious about what others see. Curious about what might be missing. Curious about whether their self-image matches reality.

Leaders who maintain that curiosity build stronger teams. Because their people know something important. Their leader is listening. Not just directing. Listening.

And when people believe their perspective matters, everything changes.

They engage more.

They speak up.

They surface problems earlier.

They take ownership of solutions.

That's when leadership stops being about control—

And becomes something much more powerful.

Shared responsibility for the mission.

Leadership Lesson

Leaders are often the last to see the true impact of their leadership.

Without honest feedback, it's easy to assume that intention equals outcome.

Strong leaders actively seek perspectives that challenge their assumptions.

Because leadership effectiveness isn't determined by how leaders see themselves—

It's determined by how their teams experience them.

The Corporate Mirror

The same gap exists in corporate environments.

Executives believe their strategies are clear.

Managers believe priorities are understood.

Organizations assume communication is effective.

But employees may experience something very different.

Unclear expectations.

Conflicting priorities.

Decisions that feel disconnected from reality.

The higher someone rises, the easier it becomes to lose visibility. Meetings become more strategic. Interactions become more formal. Information becomes filtered. And leaders begin seeing the organization through reports instead of reality.

That's when the gap widens. And if it's not addressed, performance eventually suffers.

The most effective leaders work to close that gap deliberately.

They listen.

They seek unfiltered perspectives.

They ask questions that invite honest answers.

And they stay open to the possibility that their understanding is incomplete.

When leaders operate that way, organizations change.

Communication improves.

Problems surface earlier.

Decisions become more informed.

And teams move with more confidence.

Because in the end, leadership effectiveness isn't about perception.

It's about understanding.

And the leaders who understand their people best—

Are the ones who lead them best.

Chapter 13
The Myth of the Khakis

When you're young in the Navy, the Chiefs' Mess feels almost mythical.

You hear about it before you ever fully understand it.

The khaki uniforms.
The coins.
The sayings.

"The backbone of the Navy."
"Ask the Chief."
"Trust the Mess."

For junior sailors, Chiefs seem larger than life.

They move differently.
They speak with authority.
They seem to understand how everything works.

And most importantly—

They appear to have answers.

When you're new, that kind of confidence is reassuring. The Navy is a complicated machine. Ships, aircraft, logistics systems, maintenance programs, operational schedules—none of it is simple. So when a Chief speaks with certainty, junior sailors assume that certainty comes from experience. And often, it does.

Many Chiefs earn that reputation.

They know the systems.

They know the people.

They know how to get things done.

Those are the leaders sailors remember long after the tour ends.

But as I moved through the ranks—and eventually became a Command Master Chief—my perspective started to change. Not because I lost respect for the role. Because I started seeing it from the inside. And once you see something from the inside, the mythology starts to fade.

You realize the Mess is made up of people.

Some exceptional.

Some average.

Some still figuring it out.

Just like any other group.

The khaki uniform doesn't turn someone into a leader. It marks the point where leadership responsibility increases. What someone does with that responsibility—that's what matters.

Early in my career, I believed the Mess operated as a unified body of experienced leaders guiding the command. Later, I realized it looked a lot more like any other organization.

Different personalities.

Different motivations.

Different levels of commitment.

Some Chiefs were deeply invested in their sailors. They developed people. They strengthened the command. They carried the weight of leadership the right way.

Others were more focused on themselves.

Career progression.

Visibility.

Position.

Some stayed humble and curious. Others started believing the uniform itself gave them authority that shouldn't be questioned.

That difference matters more than people think. Because when leadership cultures start focusing on symbols, they can lose sight of substance.

Coins.

Slogans.

Traditions.

They can build identity.

They can create pride.

But they don't create leadership.

Leadership requires judgment. It requires integrity. It requires the willingness to make hard decisions—and own the outcome.

Uniforms and traditions can support that. They cannot replace it.

I'll be honest. Some of the symbolism in the Chiefs' Mess always made me uncomfortable. Not the traditions themselves. Traditions matter. They connect people to history. They create continuity.

But over time, something shifted.

The coins.

The slogans.

The T-shirts.

At some point, it started to feel like the identity had become the focus.

Every season brought new coins. New designs. New sayings. New reminders of how important the Mess was supposed to be.

And I remember thinking something simple. If we have to keep telling people how important we are—We're probably focusing on the wrong thing.

Because leadership doesn't need branding. Sailors don't follow coins. They don't follow slogans. They follow leaders who make good decisions. Leaders who take care of their people. Leaders who show up when things get hard.

The best Chiefs I ever worked with didn't need to explain who they were. Their sailors already knew.

That's where the risk shows up. When organizations start confusing the symbol with the substance. When people begin to believe that wearing the uniform means the work is already done. That assumption creates blind spots. Because if the system assumes someone is already a leader, it may stop asking whether they are still growing.

Leadership development never ends. Every new role brings new challenges. New teams. New expectations.

The best leaders understand that.

They stay curious.

They keep learning.

They listen.

They adapt.

But when organizations place too much weight on identity, something else happens. Questioning becomes harder. Traditions become rules. Customs become expectations.

And leaders hesitate to challenge them—even when they know they should.

That's when mythology starts working against leadership instead of supporting it. Because strong leadership cultures should be able to examine themselves.

To ask:

Is this still helping the mission?

Or are we protecting the system?

The strongest leadership communities are the ones willing to look at themselves honestly. To recognize when something needs to change. To prioritize outcomes over identity.

At its best, the Chiefs' Mess is one of the most powerful leadership institutions in the military.

Experienced leaders supporting each other.

Sharing knowledge.

Holding standards.

Developing the next generation.

But that strength doesn't come from tradition alone. It comes from something deeper. Humility.

The understanding that leadership is never guaranteed.

It is earned—every day.

Through decisions.

Through behavior.

Through how leaders treat their people.

That's the difference. Between wearing khakis—And actually leading in them.

Leadership Lesson

Symbols can support leadership identity, but they cannot replace leadership behavior.

Strong leadership cultures focus on judgment, humility, and accountability—not just tradition or status.

Leadership is not something you achieve once.

It's something you earn, continuously.

The Corporate Mirror

Corporate organizations have their own version of khakis.

Executive titles.
Corner offices.
Reserved parking spaces.
C-suite roles.

Just like military rank, these symbols signal authority.

And just like rank, they can create the illusion that leadership automatically comes with position.

But experienced professionals know the difference.

An executive title may place someone at the top of an org chart.

It doesn't guarantee trust.

Employees watch leaders the same way sailors watch Chiefs.

They notice how decisions are made.

They notice who listens.

They notice who takes responsibility.

Those observations build reputations.

Real ones.

And those reputations carry more weight than titles ever will.

The best corporate leaders understand this.

They know authority has to be reinforced by behavior.

Every day.

Because leadership credibility isn't granted.

It's built.

Titles might open the door.

But behavior determines whether people follow you once you walk through it.

Chapter 14
The Sailors Are Always Watching

One of the most important leadership lessons I learned in the Navy is also one of the simplest.

Sailors are always watching.

Not in a suspicious way.

Not in a way that suggests they're looking for mistakes.

But they are paying attention.

To everything.

How leaders speak. How leaders make decisions. How leaders treat people. What leaders prioritize. What leaders ignore. The small moments leaders think go unnoticed are often the ones that shape how an entire command understands leadership.

Early in my career, I didn't fully appreciate that. Like most junior sailors, I was focused on doing my job, learning my trade, and staying out of trouble. Leadership existed somewhere above me.

But as I moved into leadership roles, I started noticing something.

Sailors watch closely.

They watch how leaders handle pressure.

They watch how leaders talk about the mission.

They watch how leaders treat junior sailors compared to senior personnel.

And maybe most importantly—

They watch what leaders do when nobody thinks anyone is paying attention.

Those observations build trust. Because sailors don't evaluate leadership based on speeches. They evaluate it based on patterns.

Consistency. Behavior.

If a leader talks about accountability but avoids responsibility when things go wrong—sailors notice.

If a leader emphasizes teamwork but takes credit for group success—sailors notice.

If a leader speaks about respect but treats people differently behind closed doors—sailors notice.

And those signals move fast. Often faster than any official message.

That's why leadership shows up in the small moments. Not just in crises. Not just in formal events. But in the routine interactions that define daily life.

That's also why the popcorn machine mattered. On the surface, it was nothing. Just a popcorn machine sitting in the corner of the office. But when sailors walked by and smelled popcorn, they knew something. The Command Master Chief was in. The door was open. They could stop in. Grab a bag. Talk for a minute.

Those weren't scheduled engagements.

They were small, human moments.

And sailors noticed.

They noticed that someone in senior leadership was accessible. They noticed the office didn't feel closed off. They noticed leadership didn't always exist behind a barrier.

The popcorn didn't matter.

The behavior did.

That's what leaders sometimes miss. They focus on big initiatives. Strategy. Policy. Major decisions.

Those things matter. But culture is built somewhere else.

In the hallway.

In conversations.

In how leaders respond when they're busy.

In whether they listen before they speak.

In whether they admit they don't have the answer.

Those moments send signals. And those signals add up.

When leaders show curiosity, respect, and presence, people respond. They speak up earlier. They offer ideas. They take ownership.

When leaders stay distant, something different happens. People follow instructions. But they don't go beyond them. They protect themselves. They avoid risk. And over time, the energy fades.

That's the difference.

And it doesn't come from policy.

It comes from behavior.

Because culture isn't announced. It's observed. As leaders become more senior, one thing increases quickly.

Visibility.

People notice everything.

How leaders react under pressure.

How they treat peers.

How they handle criticism.

Even tone.

Even body language.

The good news is this—Leaders don't have to be perfect. Trying to appear perfect usually creates distance.

What people respond to is consistency.

Authenticity.

Leaders who are approachable.

Leaders who take responsibility.

Leaders who show up the same way, day after day.

Because people don't trust what they're told. They trust what they see.

And sailors—like employees anywhere—are very good at seeing the truth. They pay attention because leadership decisions affect their lives. Their workload. Their opportunities. Their sense of belonging.

When leaders remember that people are always watching—not to judge, but to understand—they start leading differently.

They recognize that every interaction matters. Every decision sends a signal. Every conversation shapes perception.

And over time, something happens. The command becomes a reflection of those signals.

Not because of a slogan.

Not because of a policy.

But because of how leaders show up every day.

Leadership Lesson

Culture is built through everyday behavior.

Leaders communicate their values through what people observe—not what people are told.

Consistency, respect, and accountability create trust and initiative.

When behavior contradicts stated values, trust erodes quickly.

People believe what leaders do. Not what they say.

The Corporate Mirror

The same dynamic exists in corporate environments.

Employees are always watching.

They watch how executives respond to pressure. They notice how managers treat their teams. They pay attention to who gets credit—and who gets blamed.

Those observations shape how employees interpret company values.

Organizations publish mission statements.

Leadership principles.

Cultural guidelines.

But employees don't judge culture based on documents.

They judge it based on behavior.

If leadership talks about collaboration but rewards competition—people notice.

If leadership promotes transparency but avoids hard conversations—people notice.

Just like sailors, employees learn quickly which signals actually matter.

The strongest leaders understand this.

Culture isn't created by messaging.

It's created by behavior.

When leaders consistently demonstrate the values they expect, those values spread.

Teams mirror what they see.

Trust builds.

Initiative grows.

And the organization becomes stronger.

Not because of policy.

But because of example.

Because in every environment—military or corporate—

People are always watching.

And what they see…

Becomes the culture they believe in.

Chapter 15
After Action Report: Fatherhood

The Navy teaches you how to conduct an After Action Report.

Every operation—every exercise, every mission—eventually reaches the same moment.

The work ends.

The team gathers.

And someone asks a simple question.

How did we do?

Not the polished version. The real one. What worked. What didn't. What we would do differently next time.

Those conversations aren't about blame. They're about learning. Because organizations that don't examine their actions eventually repeat their mistakes.

The After Action Report exists for one reason—So the next mission is better than the last.

Over the course of my career, I participated in hundreds of them.

Flight operations.

Maintenance evolutions.

Deployments.

Leadership decisions.

Everything eventually came back to the same questions.

What did we learn?

What will we change?

How do we get better?

But toward the end of my career, I started realizing something.

The most important After Action Report in my life had nothing to do with a mission. Nothing to do with a command. Nothing to do with the Navy.

It had to do with being a father.

Leadership in the military is complex. It involves people, systems, missions, and responsibilities that can affect thousands of lives.

Fatherhood is different.

Two lives. Two people.

Watching everything you do—long before they understand what it means.

And in many ways, it's the most honest leadership test there is.

Because children don't care about titles. They don't care about rank. They don't care about awards or performance reports.

They care about something much simpler.

Presence.

Consistency.

Trust.

They care about whether you show up.

In the military, leadership exists inside a structure.

Policies.

Expectations.

A chain of command.

In fatherhood, the structure is simpler.

There are no formal briefings.

No evaluations.

No leadership courses.

There are only moments. Conversations. Daily interactions that shape how your children understand the world.

As my career progressed, I started seeing something clearly. Many of the lessons I learned in the Navy applied directly to fatherhood.

Not because they're the same. But because they rely on the same foundations.

Consistency.

Integrity.

Responsibility.

Children watch their parents the same way sailors watch their leaders. They notice behavior. They notice tone. They notice whether actions match words.

If you talk about honesty but act differently—they notice. If you emphasize responsibility but avoid hard decisions—they notice.

Just like sailors, children learn leadership through observation.

Not instruction.

That realization is humbling. Because it means leadership at home carries just as much weight—Sometimes more.

The difference is feedback.

In the military, results show up quickly.

Missions succeed or fail.

Teams perform or struggle.

In parenting, the feedback is delayed.

Years pass before certain lessons take hold.

And sometimes you only recognize the impact…

When your children begin navigating the world on their own.

That delay creates uncertainty.

You hope the lessons are landing.

You hope the example is clear.

But you don't always know.

That's why reflection matters.

Just like in the Navy, leadership benefits from an After Action Report.

A chance to ask:

Am I showing up the way I want my children to remember?

Am I living the values I talk about?

Am I leading with patience, curiosity, and accountability?

Or am I letting stress and distraction shape what they see?

Those questions don't require perfect answers.

But they do require honesty.

Because fatherhood—like leadership—is a continuous process of learning. Every parent makes mistakes. Every parent has moments they wish they could do differently.

The goal isn't perfection.

It's growth.

The willingness to keep learning.

To keep adjusting.

To keep showing up better than the day before.

Over time, those adjustments create something powerful.

Not just behavior—

But relationship.

Trust builds.

Respect builds.

Understanding deepens.

And eventually, the role changes.

Children grow.

They make their own decisions.

They form their own views.

At that point, leadership shifts.

From direction to influence.

From instruction to example.

And that transition felt familiar. Because it mirrors what happens in leadership roles over time.

The best leaders eventually become mentors.

Not controllers.

They create space for others to succeed. They guide when needed. But they trust the people they helped develop.

Fatherhood follows the same path. Early on, it's protection and direction. Later, it's trust and support.

And somewhere along the way, you realize something. The goal was never control. It was independence. The moment your children carry forward what they've learned—Without needing you there to guide them.

That's when the After Action Report becomes clear.

Not on paper.

But in their lives.

Their decisions.

Their character.

Their relationships.

That's the reflection.

And when you see it, you understand something that applies to every kind of leadership.

Leadership isn't about the title. Not in the military. Not in business. And not in a family.

It's about the example.

The consistency of behavior over time. The quiet signals that show people what matters.

Fatherhood strips leadership down to its core.

No slogans.

No promotions.

No recognition.

Just presence.

Just behavior.

Just impact.

And the legacy those things create.

Leadership Lesson

The most meaningful leadership influence often happens outside formal roles. Fatherhood, like leadership anywhere, is built on consistency, integrity, and example. People learn far more from what leaders do than what leaders say.

Whether leading a command, a team, or a family—

Leadership is ultimately measured by the people who grow because of it.

Epilogue

Margin for Error

Over the course of my career, I watched thousands of leadership decisions unfold.

Some were big.

Most were small.

But almost all of them came down to the same question:

Does this make the organization easier to operate—or harder?

That's the quiet reality of leadership.

Leaders don't just give direction.

They shape the environment everyone else has to operate inside.

Every rule added. Every decision delayed. Every unnecessary process created. All of it becomes weight that someone else has to carry.

Over time, I began to think about leadership the same way aviation crews think about load plans.

Every aircraft has limits.

Cargo must be balanced.

Weight distributed carefully.

Too much weight in the wrong place doesn't just make the aircraft inefficient. It makes it unstable.

Organizations work the same way.

Mission requirements add weight.

Deadlines add weight.

Limited resources add weight.

Long hours add weight.

Some of that pressure is unavoidable.

But leaders also add weight of their own.

Unnecessary rules.

Slow decisions.

Processes designed to protect appearances instead of helping people succeed.

That's where friction comes from.

And friction slows everything down.

The best leaders I served with understood something simple. Their job wasn't to control everything. Their job was to remove obstacles.

To create an environment where competent people could move quickly. Solve problems. Accomplish the mission. Without fighting the system itself.

When leaders get this right, organizations feel different.

Decisions move faster.

People trust each other more.

Energy goes toward solving problems instead of navigating bureaucracy.

When leaders get it wrong, the opposite happens.

People spend more time managing the system than doing the work.

Decisions slow down.

Frustration grows.

And eventually, the organization starts protecting itself instead of serving the mission.

Leadership will never be perfect.

There will always be friction.

There will always be competing priorities.

But the leaders who make the greatest difference usually do something very simple.

They remove the unnecessary weight.

They keep the organization balanced.

And they make it easier for good people to succeed.

If there is one idea that runs through every story in this book, it's this:

Leadership is not about adding more control. It's about knowing what weight to carry—and what weight to remove. Because every organization operates with a margin for error. And good leaders know how to protect it.

Letter to Kailey and Tiga

If you are reading this someday, it means this book actually made it into the world. That alone would surprise me a little.

Books like this are often written by people who think they have everything figured out. I never felt that way about myself. Most of what I learned about leadership came from mistakes, long nights, and the responsibility of taking care of people when things were uncertain.

For most of my adult life, I was responsible for sailors.

Young men and women who trusted me to help guide them through some of the hardest and most confusing years of their lives. I spent decades helping them navigate careers, crises, and moments when they simply needed someone older to tell them the truth.

But the two people I hoped to guide the most were always you.

Being your father has always been the most important responsibility of my life. Every promotion, every title, every command — those things mattered at the time, but they were never the real point.

You were.

And the truth is, none of it would have been possible without your mom. Koko carried a huge part of the weight while I was away serving. Military life isn't easy on families, and she gave you stability during the times when my job took me across the world on ships at sea, in Japan, and everywhere in between. For that, she deserves more credit than she'll probably ever ask for.

The Navy gave me an incredible life. It allowed me to see the world, serve alongside remarkable people, and spend most of my career in the Indo-Pacific. Japan wasn't just a duty station, it was part of your story. Kailey, you were born in Yokosuka. Tiga, you were born in Alexandria, but you only spent a short time in the United States before your life became tied to the same overseas rhythm.

But that life also meant distance.

Deployments. Long hours. Moments where I had to leave again just when things felt settled. Those are some of the quiet costs of service that people don't always see.

I hope you know that distance never meant absence in my heart.

Everything I tried to do as a leader — every sailor I mentored, every decision I made as a Command Master Chief — was shaped by the example I hoped you would see someday.

That leadership isn't about rank.

It isn't about authority.

It's about responsibility.

It's about showing up for people when it matters and carrying the weight when others can't.

If there are a few things I hope you carry forward from me, they are simple:

Be kind to people.

Work hard.

Tell the truth, even when it's uncomfortable.

And remember that the real measure of a life is not how many people worked for you, but how many people are better because you were in their life.

I am proud of both of you in ways that are hard to fully explain.

Not because of accomplishments or achievements, but because of the people you are becoming. Character is the only thing that really lasts in this world, and I have always seen that in both of you.

Whatever paths you choose, whatever lives you build, I hope you move through the world with curiosity, courage, and compassion.

If this book has any value at all, it's simply a collection of lessons from one life spent trying to lead people well.

But the truth is, the part of my life I am most proud of will never be found in these pages.

It will always be the fact that I got to be your father.

With love,

Dad

Acknowledgments

No one builds anything alone.

This book might have my name on the cover, but it was shaped by the people who stood next to me, challenged me, and trusted me over the years.

To the sailors I had the privilege to lead—this book is yours as much as mine. You were the standard. You were the reality check. You were the reason every lesson in these pages actually mattered. Leadership isn't built in offices or classrooms. It's built in moments with people—and you gave me more of those moments than I can count.

To the leaders who influenced me—good and bad—thank you. I learned just as much from what to do as I did from what not to do. To those who led the right way, you set the standard. To those who didn't, you made the lessons just as clear.

Justin, thank you for your trust, your leadership, and for being the kind of Commanding Officer who made "free chicken" make sense long before I ever thought about writing it down.

Shawn, Dean, Dan, and the people in my corner—thank you for the conversations, the perspective, and the honesty. You've all had a hand in shaping how I think, even when you didn't realize it.

To Brian, Pete, Rajeev, and Lailah—thank you for helping me adapt my leadership to a different world. The uniform changed, but the expectations didn't. Each of you pushed me to think differently, challenged assumptions, and helped me find my footing in the business environment. That perspective isn't easy to gain, and I don't take it for granted.

Koko—thank you for your support, your belief, and for the friendship we've built over time. Not everything in life follows a straight path, but the respect and trust we've maintained means a lot to me.

Dad—Rick—you've always been my biggest fan. The one posting old Navy pictures, telling people stories, and probably bragging about me more than I ever would myself. I don't say it enough, but it means more than you know. A lot of who I am—and how I lead—started with you.

And to my kids, Kailey and Tiga—everything comes back to you.

This book is a reflection of what I learned over a lifetime of leading people, but more than that, it's a record of what I hope you carry forward. Not the titles, not the positions—but the way you treat people, the way you show up, and the way you lead when it actually matters.

If this book does anything right, it's because of the people in it.